transcona fragments

transcona fragments

poems by Jon Paul Fiorentino

Copyright © 2002 Jon Paul Fiorentino

All rights reserved. No part of this book may be reproduced by any means–graphic, electronic or mechanical–without the prior written permission of the publisher or author, without the exception of brief passages in reviews, or for promotional purposes.

Printed and bound in Canada

Cover and book design: Rayola Graphic Design
Photos courtesy of the Chudley family archive

CANADIAN CATALOGUING IN PUBLICATION DATA

Fiorentino, Jon Paul, 1975 –
Transcona Fragments
Poetry.
ISBN 1-894177-11-8

1. Title.
PS8561.I585T73 2002   C811'.6   C2002-900948-0
PR9199.4.F56T73 2002

Represented in Canada by the Literary Press Group
Agented by Signature Editions
Distributed by General Distribution Services

The publisher and author gratefully acknowledge the financial assistance of the Manitoba Arts Council and the people of Manitoba.

Cyclops Press
P.O. Box 2775
Winnipeg, MB R3C 4B4 Canada
www.cyclopspress.com
www.jonpaulfiorentino.com

For Onofrio, Cheryl, James, Georgina, Nadia and Tara

"transcona fragments" was first published in *You and Your Bright Ideas: New Montreal Writing*. Véhicule Press, 2001. "trance/coma" was first published in *dark leisure, volume 2*. "the residents of st. james" was first published in *Prairie Fire*, 20:2. "prairie long poem" was first published in *Headlight Anthology, volume 3*.

Thanks to Chandra Mayor, Sarah Steinberg, Geoff Lansdell, Manon Christina Palassio, Kate Hall, Chris Charney, Terry Watts, Leigh Scharnik, Chrystal Staver. Special thanks to Robert Budde, Mary di Michele, Catherine Hunter, Clive Holden. Very special thanks to Tara Flanagan for her brilliance, patience and love.

scales   9

section 1 : transcona fragments
transcona fragments   13
trance/coma   15
recess   25
floodway dream   28
queen's court   29
transcona cemetery   39

section 2 : psychotropes
dopamine song   49
psychometrics   50
psychotropes   51
ventolin   62
used bell jar   65

section 3 : the residents of st. james
the residents of st. james   73
marker   75
hole   77
fluorescence   78
letter to sarah   81
dishappy   83
spectre   84

ember	87
tenemental	88
ex. hail.	90
interlake	92
prairie long poem	94

scales

if you spend all your time on social skills
then you will never learn your scales

practice opening those gilded wounds
amid the feedback of a trebled night that you fail to notice

from beneath your oversized quilt
stuck within the veiled dreams of others and Other

scales are made to break you, to make you
accept the enforced synchronicity of things

trickle on plastic strings or faux ivory keys
take a textbook to bed in your closet

wrap yourself in sheet music
proceed parental empirical funereal

strike those chords that don't quite fit infuse sharp
or descend flat into outside   home

twitch, tap virginal as the children play the street to death
ascending toward song, silently trampling

casting dead monitor-grey shadows
across your living room and your laboured music

listen to what you can do because no one else will
everyone is neatly placed in freon

you are stuck in a metronome
feebly clicking, swaying

on a typical soundproof summer day
you break under an off-white ceiling, dreaming in vivid blue

section 1
transcona fragments

> *When we met in the street the houses had grown sombre. The space of sky was the colour of ever-changing violet and towards it the lamps of the street lifted their feeble lanterns.*
> —James Joyce

transcona fragments

ah good old ground tasting like invasive snow
salt reeling under exhaust (no matter the cost)
and don't forget to write from the east where
you will sit in a state of abandoned bliss stitched
to a street that hardly knows you

unpacking that metaphor the unkempt gravel
or tar of a transcona side street driving with your
third eye on the road splaying yourself out the side
window, with both eyes on what you know

that taste, that region: gravel, tar, spit leaves
of glass splinters on the dream road tin am radio
chevrolet and a block heater and an electric blanket
and a six pack for christmas

park on the frigid plain, dig a ditch round the city
plunge into floodway and dream headlong into traffic
as if you had the guts as if you ever had
the pleasure

under windows laced with the thickest frost
you ramble on about the weather and the family
and i'm almost lured into your language until i recoil
at the irrational flash of a police search light

we quickly clothe ourselves and turn down the heater
and turn up the radio and pretend to be innocents with
decorative smiles for the constable who was hoping
for something more cinematic

trance/coma

nairn overpass—
a slide into toxins

i collect everything i choke on
        never choke on substance
i never write about transcona
        never
but this summer
full of sick collectable sewage
finds me with something
to write about
and i don't have to rename it
(but i probably will)

understand this—
        rain is
        an elusive character
        promising to lubricate the descent
        into transcona
        but failing to make it any easier

      home is only paper
      containing a flatland sermon

      rain tapping on our vehicle
      on the nairn overpass

hydroplaning
      the downward slope
      despite the impossibility
      of bridging the gap
      between dimensions
      and ourselves

        transcona is not sicker
        quicker than any other
        suburban subtext
        in subversive verse
        but transcona has/had history
        that does/did not elude me

so truly i write to you—
        transcona wakes with mourning sickness
        and the embryonic mornings
        are like sorrowful sermons
        our sorrow-filled ascent into winnipeg
        is not any better than the evening slide
        but it is different
        the morning is at least cold with difference
        differing and deferring
        and we—
        in our ascent
        (for want of a better way)
        can say
        good morning to an urban illusion

and negotiate
an urbane intrusion
between threads
that resemble
the thoughts surrounding
dimensionality

again traveling home
mouthing the music silent
slippery again
raining again
overpass
and
afterthought

beginning
descent

descending
a train begins
and draws itself a story
dissecting transcona smoothly

        how long can this train last?
        you don't answer
        you're not really here

know this—
        rain is a colour-enhancing trickster
        outside our vehicle, seeping though a cracked window
        a train is holding us from being held hostage

transcona makes me lie
> converts me through silent sermons
> exhaust toxins coffins
> my grandfather buried here—
> 1983
> lies
> to me/for me
> and i suspect
> he still chokes on dust
> from time to dilated time

> *you see over there?*
> *that gravestone with my family name?*
> *that's my grandfather under erasure*
> *that's where he writes those poems*
> *that challenge the very notion of time*

of course we are at a distance and we can't read the gravestone from the highway
but i think you get the general idea
this is friction

transcona is perhaps not the epicentre of things:
dust
cemeteries
rain
dimensions
scattered abstractions
but then again

and coming to transcona is never really coming or going

to tell the truth
> it is not really a descent
> from the top of the nairn overpass
> to the depths of illness and collected toxins

to tell the truth
it is an interactive
trance/coma

recess

for Leigh Scharnik

all children but two
are tethered to the asphalt
under supervised derision

twinned boys are hiding
under unsafe slides stealing
moments together

they sit, sift in winter sand and
conjure up shame in their heads over
and over as if they are tethered
to the fear of desire come here

and they slide into the backlanes that lace
the schoolyard, sparking on the frigid
ground with pockets full of bottlecapped
oil sucking it all in before the principal hears
about their absence

on the school grounds:
a frayed rope passed out
a lethargic flag just sagging

and the boys rest on oil-soaked
clouds under a dormant truck

don't say a word i
hear the footsteps
hear the voices
adult and symphonic
the lonely teachers are
marching and chattering
in tangible rhythms
let's sleep this
day to memory
in the shadows
let's fuse
hypothermic
tether ourselves to ourselves

floodway dream

the dream is a lucite window

last night i dreamt i brought you and your partner (staying at my old
house at 189 allenby
crescent, transcona, manitoba, canada) a newly hatched
mallard or whatever it was that i found at the floodway
(of course, i have never met your partner
so she wore a television face)

another section of the dream
(put together in fragmented pastiche)
was a film narrative in which you and i were shooting
rubber bullets at tenements and breaking into
bungalows and the transcona historical museum

there were vintage hockey cards littered along the floodway in terrible
condition—
no lucite, no value

queen's court

the telephone poles are
the tallest structures here—
pillars of dull luminosity
cheap amber street light
encasing this community
frigid stems suggesting *stay here*
blowing snow dancing in electric ribbons
gravel roads and pale voices laced with poison

and oh
christ the flicker
of lethargic neon
in a goddamned
ghost town
there is a
cryogenic memory
twitch in that hollow street
where the queen's court
used to sit always
slanting toward
the east

within spitting distance
the transcona historical museum
holds fast to the corner
of bond and regent holding
its archival bliss
resisting the urge
to keel over

stand up straight

hangover boy
in your unremarkable bedroom
you fail to sleep in this
frigid early morning
you are guided by
memory in the
luminosity
of winter

this morning
a glint of light
fails to wake
a frostbitten man
twitching in a ditch
half covered by dead snow
yet synthetically warm
thanks to a homemade bottle

above him at the side of the road
is a sign: Welcome to Transcona

the sun rises over
a suburban scene
the scene takes years
the bungalows are patient

the silent streets glisten
laced with black ice
amber streetlights
automatically dying
as day breaks

hangover boy, you whimper in your sleep:
all the houses here are the same
you plant yourself into your pillow
your head is heavy
with the appalling
science of self

and it's true hangover boy—
all the houses here are the same
but the queen's court was unique and you breathe in
its disordered ghosts whenever you pass out on the asphalt
(which you always do)
or when your body delicately meets with hardwood and you
realize that you live on a slant
(and you always will)

stand up straight

notes from the Transcona Historical Museum with interruptions

      The Queen's Court was demolished in 1973.

that was two years before you were born
but you somehow remember it—
the hardwood, the hallways and rooms marked with the same sour scent
the tenants slack under the permanent deconstruction:
the lazy creak under feet
the hardwood lunging toward
the ground, praying for burial

      The Queen's Court stood on the corner of Regent and
      Winona.

you found out that your great-grandmother considered the queen's
court one of her very favourite old haunts and this gave you temporary
chills but you don't believe in hauntings
(and you never will)

still you know despite the absence of photographs, the absence of logic, and the overwhelming intimate knowledge of construction, you swear you were there trying to negotiate that particular slant of the second floor, almost there, almost home

hangover boy, i know it doesn't make much sense but if you just let go and accept then perhaps you can begin to try to decode this

and today
the storefronts beg you to go away
to forget their constant reinventions
and hollow conventions of retail

the hardware store begat the used book store begat the sports card store begat the video store

meet me in the middle of the street just about now
let the feeble tinge of home glint off of the
hardened snow

let the fields sparkle like lamé
let our breath meet in the sky under
the unremarkable undulation of northern lights

here is the park you never played in:
the skeletal trees whisper
leave while you can
but you don't believe in belief

in your dreams
your great-grandmother spits on her welcome mat
and takes a long swig of a favourite poison, sinks into her
mattress and fails to remember to dream

and what is your poison?
which way do you sway
when you try your very best to forget?

The Queen's Court. est. 1909 Thomas Envoy Prop.
    233 Regent Ave West.
    62 Rooms. A saloon full of empty.
    A railway town full of half full bodies.
    The place to be in Transcona or even Winnipeg!
    (The saloon was called The Bucket of Blood.)

you are searching for a place to be
certain of breath, consumption
and anger

you live in a region so starved of anything real
that you have to fictionalize history in your dreams

in the distanced present, a school bell rings
and children begin to cross streets, negotiate
the sparse traffic, a stunted boy
somehow manages to distinguish
his house from all the others
just like you used to

> The Queen's Court was taken apart in stages. First the roof and balcony were lowered to the ground like a corpse, last rites clanking and screeching within machinery or whispered from the sidewalk by a fading railwayman holding an empty pint glass. Then the headless building grew colder. The prairie sky was red velvet.

your great-grandmother had her
picture taken mid-demolition
posing as a spinster, hard-faced
yet emoting a perverse obligation
to home

and now you retreat to a bed
in another city in the same routine
of ineffective forgetting

somewhere between homely and homing
you recover in stages a pixelated history:
dreams of weathered pictures
of telephone poles, or blowing
snow flickering like tinsel

one day you will wake up
and set off for queen's court
everyone needs somewhere
to spit

transcona cemetery

consider these
plastic flowers
that we stole from the cemetery
so we could place them on rusting cars
on bleached suburban nights

the seamless dignity of our youth
and place as if regent avenue was
ste. catherine or even wimpole street

you would never meet me with your hands
you were busy clasping spray paint or stencils
i could never take my eyes off your hands
bleached with your work

your metallic eyes lost in me
lost on me your gaunt skin tinged with rust
your ability to reason blooming

consider these plastic flowers shooting out of our back pockets, bending feebly toward each other, wavering in an unremarkable evening, and we were testing car doors or engaging in the marking of the universe, a universe as regional as a sublimated clasp as seamless as simple theft

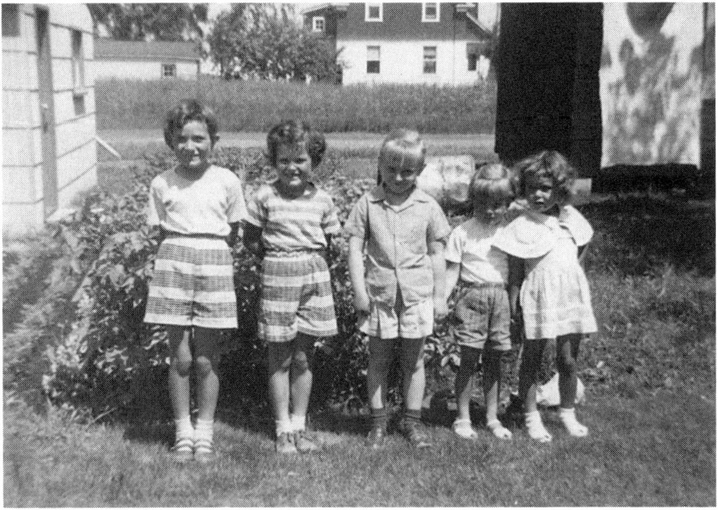

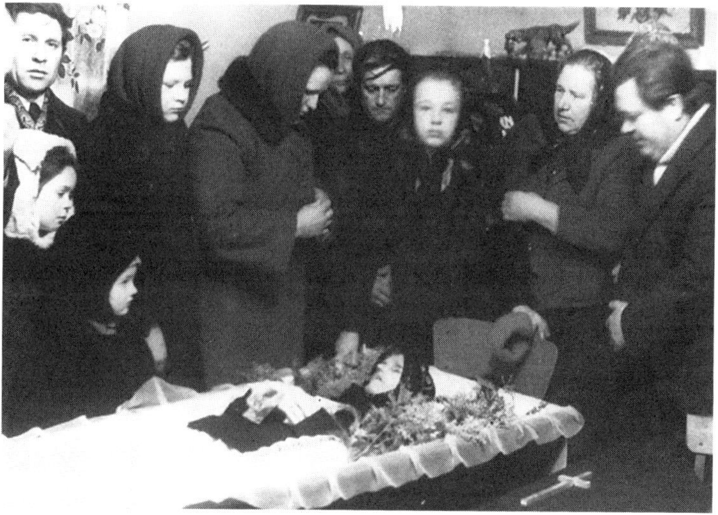

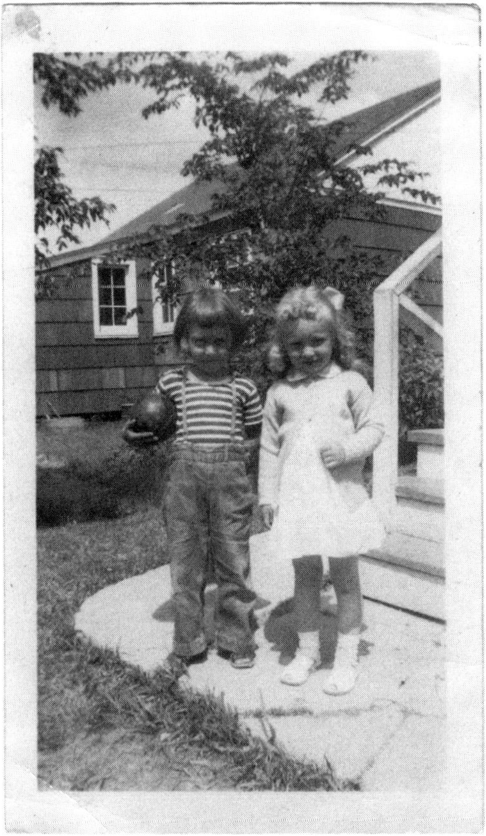

AUG 1960

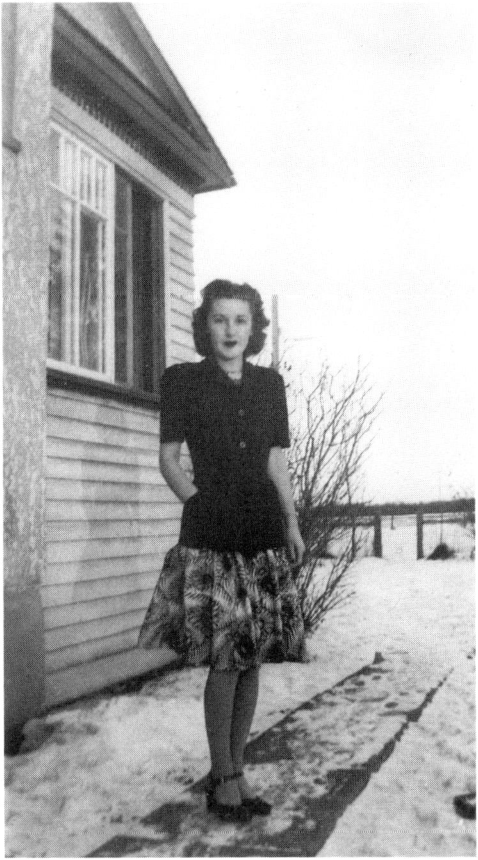

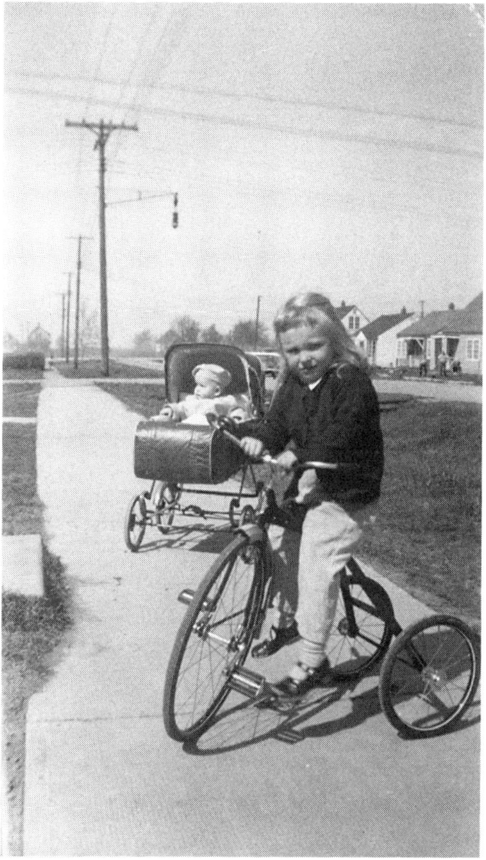

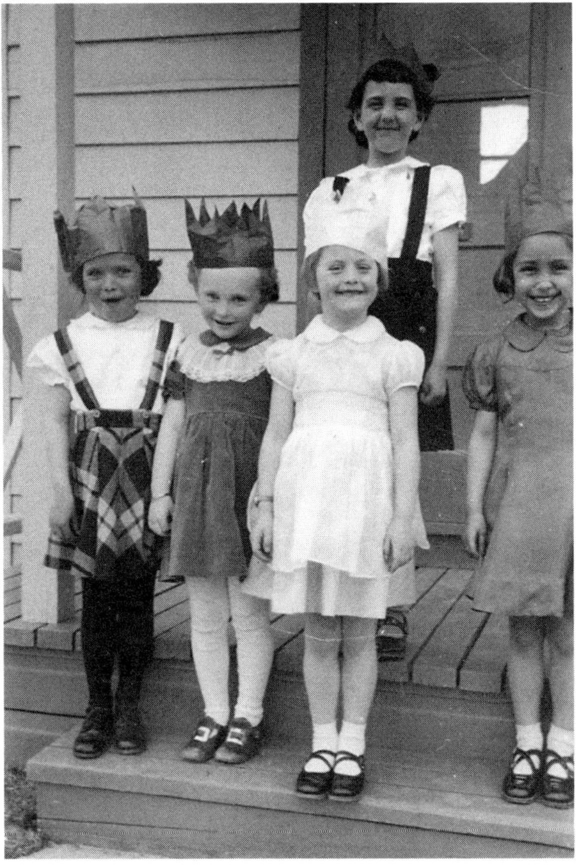

section 2

psychotropes

but calming, slipping back into silence. sighing, "i"
—Robert Budde

dopamine song

dream, cut the tether
split the skin just there and let
everything thrum within your pale
body

trill in that kinetic moment, let
that reverb last, plunge into the
bathtub

colour the water, create
snap your neck along the ceiling

stain the walls with your
winter, taste thrush and don't
forget   to breathe

let the neurons fire, mis-
fire and where are you now?

underdressed with a tourniquet
in adrenaline verse, or slamming
your way into sleep again?

psychometrics

can only dream in certain psychometrics make
believe downpour and circumvent grammar
eyes always make turn away faces
pale grey pills and absentee pronouns

roll calling and naming and missing
hymn stealing a rhythm to come into
own down whisper basement don't
give away psyche or order imperative

marginal taste fervour devour suggest
not the firmament spread out like praxis
eyes that flicker dream sublimate and
can only watch metre like a paralytic

the eyes are yours they turn away like
passengers carrying on without you
and i watch you inattentive come home
calling dream certain windows certain
pills certain minor chords certain rules
certain signs assigned and subverted

you.
present.

psychotropes

if you wade through
this space called home
you will find
it is marked with
spiritual alcohol networks
abandoned performative waste

this space called home
is the cell you will study
the microscopic ghost
replicating through mitosis

in this space called home
you will
        wade
        swim
         strategically
         drown

in an
        exhaust
        oxygen

        alcohol
        ocean

you will surface
clinging to
        invisible
        miserable
        psycho
        tropes

you will pass
these bottled spirits around
with a grand molecular gesture

you were wading through
this space called home
and you came across the razor
that lusted after your wrists

when you were young
you used to
spit and slip and slit

                              now you refrain and you write and you fail

this razor was a blank page
but you longed to bleed poetry all over
its dull rusty terrain

you longed to break the blood down
into phonemes and morphemes
read each monosyllabic cell

you longed to make a language
of abstractions and psychotropes
an asylum for unwanted metaphors

you don't like this do you?
i don't blame you

negative drown multiplied by negative drown
equals positive hover

there is potential
in this space called home
to achieve weightless grace
or at least expire like metre

the illuminated hallway seeps into the room filled with white gauze and
sleepless nurses

finally
she finds a source
she finds a vein

this is not the clinic
this is the psychiatry ward
she wants to search your blood
she wants to purge your blood

"we believe you have an abnormally high psychotrope count—
a figurative chemical imbalance"

beneath your skin
microscopic
gravity
dancers
literal
free
radicals
in
positive
hover

"please consider . . .
> neurotransmitter
>> re-uptake
>>> inhibitor . . ."

take these pills
with solids

nothing is solid
atoms in transient bonds

"please consider . . ."

psychotrope attack
where is your pen
> paper
> liquid
> solid
> lattice
> uptake
> re-uptake

take these pills (for granted)

        don't swallow
                whole
        don't swallow
                here
        don't swallow
                now
if you swallow you will drown
                      don't drown

there is a concrete metaphor on your horizon
let it grip you like causal gravity
allow difference
into your
bloodstream
because
all that is left
in your veins
is broken glass

and all that you own is a razor
and an empty oxygen tank

the ward is full
        psychotropes are spreading in ink like a glacial sidewalk

and the world is full
        with poets
        coming

this is about how you fend off every virus with this illness

and yes
this is about the razor
and the space called home
and drowning
and coming

        overcoming

this is about the psychotropes you know
and knowing you know them—
you know that you don't

this is about waiting past the wading

and you come, overcome, become

sinking into the sidewalk
psychotropic body stone
ethereal wordscaping
fixture is drowning
in sidewalk

at home
you are dreaming of my sidewalk
descending, emoting my uptake
wounds seamlessly unfolding
cold sweat speaking of my sidewalk
etching sores into a sublimated bedpost

this is really about the broken bottles
whether they contained alcohol or pills
prescribed or imbibed

this is about the oxygen tank

this is about the razor
and the shattered glass
in your veins you
keep coming
and coming
back to the
page

ventolin

i need you like ventolin or autumnal notions that comfort spastic

sighs, breath

you lure me inward like lethargic dreams   plural scenes

i wheeze through bluescreen emotions
                               (the television flickers just right)
i gaze through the blue gauze of intensive care
or sputter after   every second ember
sparking up despite the weather   a sad smoking asthmatic
this bland and still november   will be a highly suspect trope

       work it out on your own

here i am pacing through mirror stages

                                                   under weeping glucose
in and out as inpatient

shuffling through the halls with oxygen companion
rolling my eyes with the nurses of st. boniface

                                       posing with intravenous and you
intensive care—i live here intensively

i dream on a nauseating street while pedestrians squirm their way to work
i'm dreaming you over
come on over

ventolin reminds me to breathe

                                    takes me under the discursive surface

    tripping on a stream   life is a dream trope

ventolin: treatment of in contemporary personal narrative

prescriptions are meant to be filled

but this november it might be nice to breathe the air that

lingers just above my sickly street, to swallow icy exhaust

and see what happens with each and every pixel of you

there's a lie   i like to dream   in unmetered lines

                                    i'm sleeping out of breath

this november will be different—

    carefully edited   delicate spacing and breathing

just under your breath

november—will it ever come?

used bell jar

i bought *the bell jar*
at a used book store
the book seemed fine
for one dollar twenty five

i thought the pages were clean
like neatly pressed dresses
with dreams stitched in

but when esther came home
there was alien ink in the margins
sick shorthand stains
traces of water

paper
an old woman's
yellow skin
wrinkled
translucent
exposing
veins

when i woke with esther
after the pills betrayed us
the pages were stuck together
and the delicate surgery
that severed these bonds
revealed insects
dead little esthers in stasis
like accidental auras
or
us

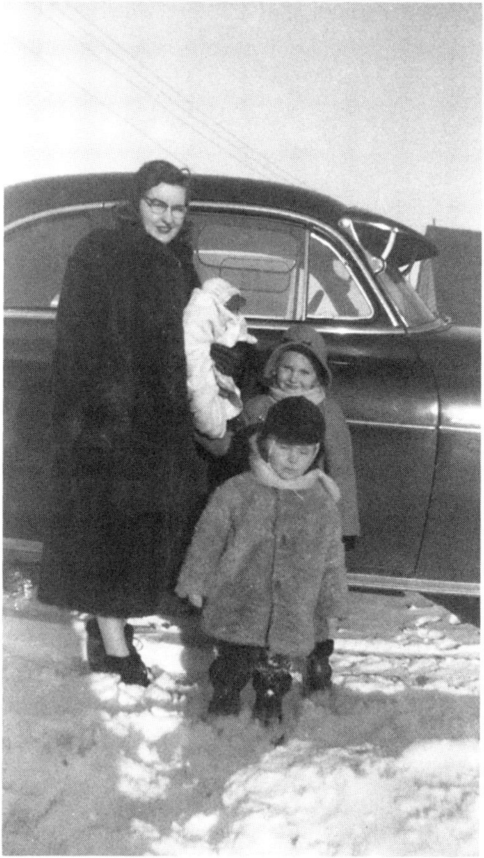

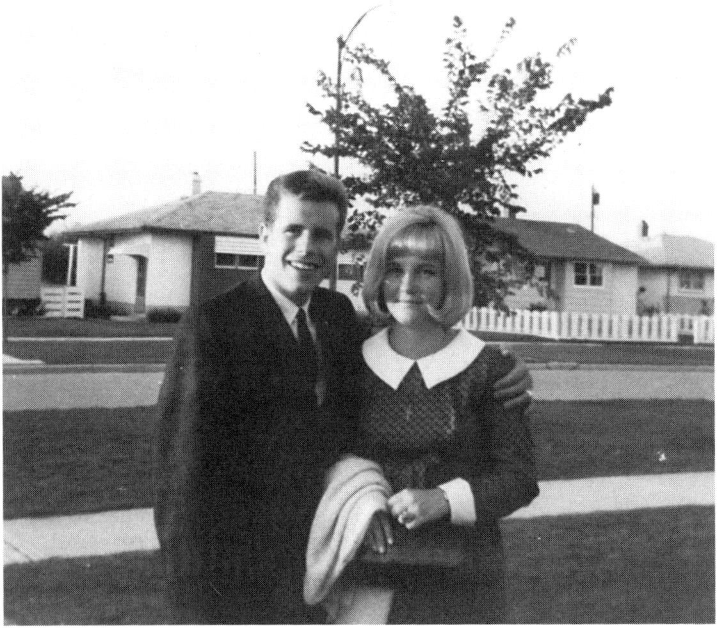

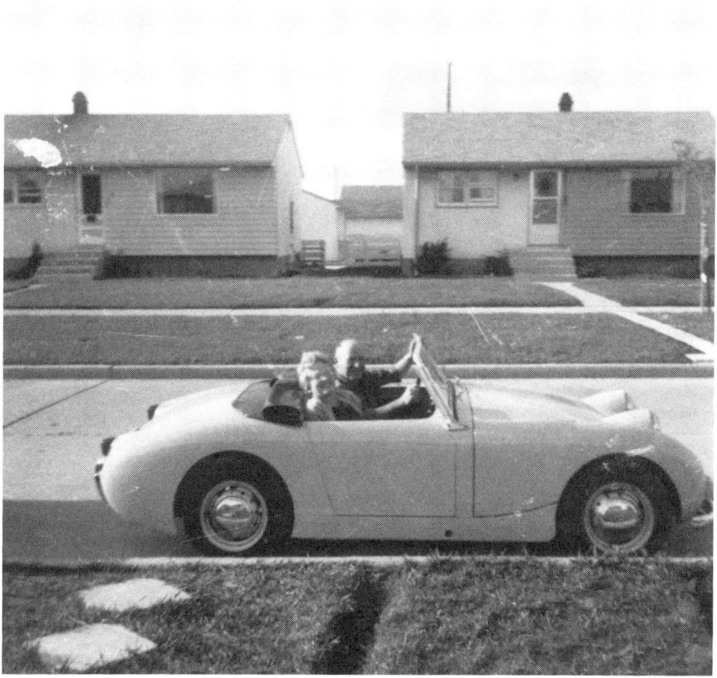

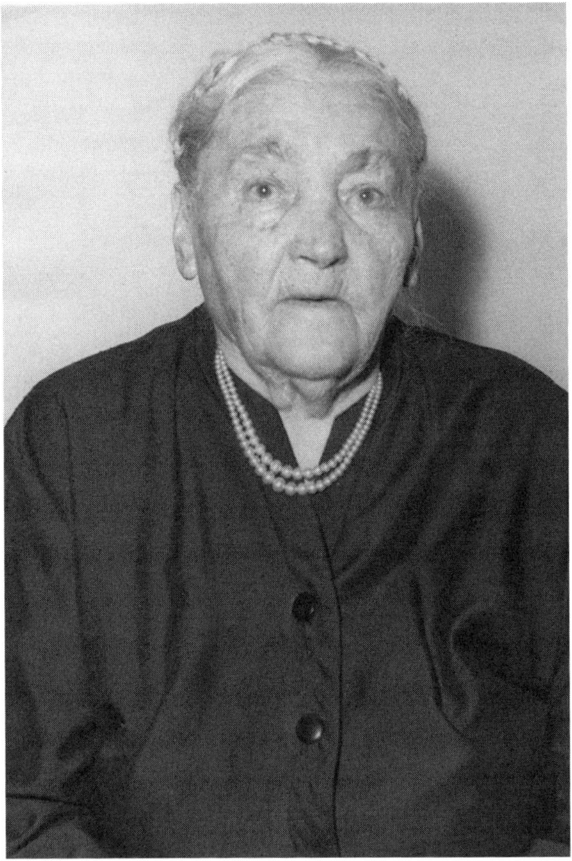

section 3

the residents of st. james

> *reality is a bit of chalk*
> *traces without tracing*
> *life, its deciphering*
> *in blue the shadow of narratives*
> *reality always exists*
> *elsewhere*
>
> —Nicole Brossard

the residents of st. james

i had a tylenol breakfast this morning
the residents of st. james were still sleeping
i browsed through their tool shack secrets and early morning sins
from my window
i got bored
i browsed through the book that i own
i am certain that one day
i'll build up the courage
to steal a new one
as long as it's not a poetry book
there are too many
about god and satan and zeus and athena and so on
and there are not enough about andy kaufman
and not enough are andy kaufman
i stopped at the local whatever
and finished my valium lunch

i never start
the things that i finish
and this is why everything's already done

the residents of st. james are still sleeping
in my own way i have tried to wake them

marker

we tried the cathedral in st. boniface
but it was already occupied
with the trace of alcohol
and the promise of violence

so something took us
to assiniboine park
and our bodies hovered over the path
avoiding the sick lovers

i saw you cringe
as i used my permanent marker
to ask you a question

and the sidewalk shook
as you answered
in my language
with a timid ink accent

you wrote our entire story:
YES
you are sick
YES
you are permanently marked
YES
you
YES
you
YES

hole

in the corner of the hole he whispered a static "no."
she pushed him into traffic

and he was haloed and sober yet disoriented
the night called him names the sky ceased its gaze
he fell beneath a moving truck carrying useless family
chests and stressed cardboard boxes containing photographs
and hardcover books and costume jewelry and she whispered
a frenetic "yes."

never leave the hole
never find yourself
impossibly cornered

fluorescence

i fluoresce
with certain conditions
in a self-contained
radiation-ready
text

there i am—
a photosensitive boy
on your driveway
gendering myself
with a pen
making my chemistry real
adding erasure to taste

of course
it is night
and i am sleepstalking
sweetly

chanting lyrics in a fluorescent
anti-lyrical tongue

there i am—
that little radiant insect

seducing our teenage trace to life
on the driveway your father paved

there is no radiation
that isn't in some way
contained

fluorescence is the dream i write
from photosensitive solace
and deliver to your driveway at 3am
under the guise of night—
containment

there is no radiation
that doesn't
escape

letter to sarah

if you find you
have the time
write a book about yourself entitled
"ideology boy"

skip yourself tonight, get lost in your sewing
or hang yourself from your answering machine
with silver thread, don't erase the messages

re-record your self and welcome home

pose amid the throes of self-actualization
for fuck's sake roll your eyes until they
roll over and then change your price

the measurements should be 6 X 4—a pocketbook that
would fit neatly in the pocket of a thrift polyester jacket, size 42 regular

perhaps a matte cover and humourless faux biography of the author
and a novelty photo of a starlet in place of a photo of you

oh, and we miss you—some of us have slid into your apartment in the early morning and read the contents of your fridge and others have fictionalized you with analogue fervour and wrote emotive verse with thin-tipped black markers on napkins and the ink leaked everywhere, staining everything

yours,

dishappy

it's 4 am
all the dealers have gone home
to their bungalows

and the night is blowing holes
through its endless supply of grey matter

every door is locked

the muses are hooked on retail, window
shopping under filthy streetlights

every shot is muted

in the industrial parks, the children are sleeping
endeavouring toward a gentle apnea, wavering between
condensation and displacement

everyone dishappy

spectre

for John K. Samson

winnipeg's restored district:
never tear down any building lucky enough to be haunted

a notion disperses like a scattered pamphlet—
home is where you are discarded

singular and here, traffic lights changing
as quickly as your mind, the lethargic wind
coiling around the streetlight, a nondescript
dancer drafted against the pull of
a home dis-
choreographed

the snake-like curl of your unkempt hair, your
dirty guitar strings, the grime beneath your
fingernails, your countless hardwood cells, you're
sure that you will leave, as if leaving means
anything other than
absence

the sweet threat of continuing to breathe, of not
giving in to giving, those exchange district buildings
with their terrible posture are posing again
frozen, stillborn, unwashed and
photogenic

the wind whips through albert street like a vitriolic
lecture, the children are paralytic and without
speech, enveloped in spray paint and precious words
tagging themselves smothering the structures
statuesque against dirty, pretty, crooked
walls

the empty restaurant with a neatly placed bullet hole
in the window, the artspace building emptying its
contents onto the cobblestone, one notion just
scattered and trampled under a lazy rush hour
breathless pedestrians, sporadic swarm
billowed breath dancing above street level
the young girl practicing widowing
with pale blue chalk on the sidewalk

you are almost there now—

ember

it was the ember that coerced the morning out of its coma
        the filthy illumination of toxin land, jaundiced dust
                the damp asthmatic filter of here, tourists pasted to hotel windows
        the grainy waves of petrol, the empty convenience stores
it was the ember that sparked your coughing fit, your blood vessels opening
        your bruised face the colour of an alcohol-drenched sky
you stood there like a dying fire, talking yourself to sleep
slouching on the sidewalk, carrying a leaking pen and receipts to scrawl on
it was the ember that tripped you, tripped your breath and allowed this day to begin
        oil stains all over the sidewalk, a map all over your face

that ember that dropped into grey from your ash-tipped fingers
that meaning that feeling that descended all over the place

tenemental

living here is very tenemental
don't come down from the lattice

scale the structure instead, an insect
inside the inside of a home
ascend
it's a very
very very
nice view

etchings you've never seen
buildings you've never known
someone unlatches himself from a door
on the verge of turning the knob
and presenting himself to the hallway
someone calls home from home
someone can only remember your number
by looking at the numbers, give him a rotary
phone and watch him sink

        you and your perverse hailings:
dial. dial. dial.

take the numbers off your door   you are not home
crash beneath the sink
step off the balcony, breathe in a little rust, leaves of paint
sign a lease, light a candle, paint a wall, fashion a noose, pay a bill or two, make some new clothes
reconnect the phone, dial from memory

the building is slouching toward the east
the power is out again

ex. hail.

when you were a young adult
someone firebombed your apartment
block as if someone important was living
there, they dreamt you into a tirade
you were waving, wavering on
your crooked balcony, the firefighters
didn't even acknowledge you

behind the apartment block:
piss-stained sofas
fridges and rusted grates
a shadow trading his memory
for a coin or two, tracing his
history through the lattice
of an abused shopping cart
a subtle billowing ascending
in asphalt grey

once, a city bus crashed into a neighbouring
building while you were out being
neighbourly, the city woke for a moment

the elevator was in flux and the
heating ceased, you exhaled as
if you were on vacation, as if you could

some nights, you sleepwalk to the balcony
grip the rusty rail with one hand and
wave with the other

if anyone is around
they might notice you
but you are too busy
inhaling and exhaling
to notice
anything

interlake

i buried you
out in the interlake
out where the stars breathe
out where the invalid snow rests
like weighted paper

i married you
out in the interlake
out where the stars grow
out of thick red soil

this is where i placed you
this is all about bringing
you somewhere to rest
ending that frigid
dream of belonging

out where the
winter steals
my oxygen
i buried you
breathless
i married you
senseless

prairie long poem

i have read *seed catalogue* and *the wind our enemy* and *fielding* and still i will fail to present you with this prairie long poem because if anything they have taught me to write against this form and to be discursive and elusive and most of all they have taught me to desire each other and so to perpetuate an incestuous notion of poetry which is discretely referred to as intertextuality.

write fragments. not full sentences. but most of all disobey all instructions toward poetry.

"son this is a modem
    this is a wordprocessor
    this is a concrete metaphor
    this is a sledgehammer"

"and the next time you want to write a poem we'll start praying"

the first thing i remember about winnipeg is the king's head pub and the people i dragged there in order to sap them of poetic energy like an alcoholic parasitic hybrid of student and sociopath.

the first thing i remember about winnipeg is the womb and the poetry i radiated within while sucking on a fort garry ale and looking for a hookup.

right on motherfucker hook me up—
two for twenty-five? i love you man.

let's walk through the cinematically static exchange district and discuss the meaning of staticity and let's walk closer to our surroundings. don't detach yourself from the possibilities here in this barren city as infertile as the surrounding land yielding and yielding and yielding words.

i have been on a farm (just once) and i was disobedient—i read kroetsch again while the others engaged in a profound (mis)understanding of their immediate surroundings.

the immediacy of space wasted on me as I decided to distance myself and I became i.

aborting a landscape.

"and the next time i want to read a poet i'll start unnaming" print me oh prairie long poem with your mythological power and your subversive subnature and i will be forever ungrateful like a spoiled prairie child who has only seen history from the back seat of his parents' car, his eyes peering over the limits of the child safety window.

print me in colour, defiant and disobedient to the word "color" and the absence of you.
print me canadian like an alcoholic king's head patron mouthing to the clash through the stifling ambience of menthol cigarette smoke and echoing pick up lines.

print me in technicolo(u)r as an obscure reference to my conventionally contemporary attention span and my desire spanning from the airwaves of broadcast to the incestuous, claustrophobic, surge of cable.

print me oh print me in winnipeg: home of the wholesale poet and the alcoholic.

imprint me like the inward surge of metonymy and philosophical metaphor.
imprint me oh prairie long poem

      through incestuous academy

                          and frostbitten home.